Come Away My Beloved!

Keys to Cultivating a Life of Intimacy with God.

by David Mayorga

SHABAR PUBLICATIONS

www.shabarpublications.com

Most Shabar Publications products are available at special quantity discounts for bulk purchase for sales promotions, fund-raising and educational needs. For details, write Shabar Publications at mayorga1126@gmail.com.

Come Away My Beloved! *Keys to Cultivating a Life of Intimacy with God* by David Mayorga

Published by Shabar Publications
3833 N. Taylor Rd.
Palmhurst, Texas 78573
www.shabarpublications.com

Unless otherwise noted, all Scripture quotations are from the New Kings James Version of the Bible. Copyright@1979, 1980, 1982 by Thomas Nelson, Inc., publishers. Used by permission.

ISBN 978-1-955433-13-6

Note: This publication contains the opinions and ideas of its author(s). It is intended to provide helpful and informative material on the subject matter covered. It is sold with the understanding that the author(s) and publisher are not engaged in rendering professional service in the book. If the reader requires personal assistance or advice, a competent professional should be consulted. The author(s) and publisher specifically disclaim any responsibility for any liability, loss, or risk, personal or otherwise, which is incurred as a consequence, directly or indirectly, of the use and application of any of the contents of this book.

Table of Contents

Foreword

'LIFE' is a result of intimacy. Not only is that true in the natural but also in the spiritual realm.

God's word uses the term *knew* to describe sexual intercourse between a husband and his wife. Jesus stated to the false prophets that He *never knew* them. This word *knew or know,* suggests more that just a casual understanding of someone or something. To say you *know* your spouse and also your bank teller, would suggest two radically different levels of knowledge. God desires us to *know Him* in a deep, personal and intimate way.

The Christian life is compared to many things throughout God's word. We are called sheep, temples, buildings, vessels, epistles, fields, children, stones, etc. However, the one description that trumps them all is that of *a bride*.

As Christians we are called into a deep, personal relationship with God that will eventually result in our eternal marriage to our heavenly Bridegroom and glorious Savior, King Jesus.

The book you hold in your hands, was written for the sole purpose of instructing and encouraging you on how to deepen your relationship with the Living God.

Jesus described 'eternal life' not simply as a decision made at some church altar or in some arena months or years ago, but rather ... Well let's read exactly what Jesus said: **"And this is eternal life, that they may *know Thee*, the only true God, and Jesus Christ whom Thou has sent."** (John 17:3)

Eternal life is more than just a decision; it's a new desire, not for sin, but for God Himself. The Apostle Peter compares it to the desire of a new born baby for it's mother's milk.

No matter how long your first date may have been, I can guarantee that if you were smitten in any way with the one you were with - you were already desiring to see that person again and again and again. How much more our eternal Lover and Savior, the Lord Jesus Christ.

In this much needed book, David Mayorga lays out the necessary steps to cultivate a personal and intimate relationship with Christ. Like any relationship the more time you invest in it the more of a reward you will receive from it.

One of the signs Jesus gave of His soon coming return not only included wars and rumors of wars, earthquakes and pestilence etc., but the fact that the love of many would grow cold.

As in all relationships they need to be maintained. Failure to do so leads to complacency, compromise, concupiscence which results in caring and caressing someone or something else. It may not always be another person.

Demas, one of the Apostle Paul's co-workers left the ministry due to his overwhelming love for the world. It could also be the love of money that eventually wins out over our love for Christ; and so for that reason, we need to fervently guard our hearts. We do this by spending time daily in God's presence and His Word.

I have told countless young people entering the ministry that the key to their effectiveness, is through cultivating a daily quiet-time with the Lord. After all, the first and foremost commandment is **'YOU SHALL LOVE THE LORD YOUR GOD WITH ALL YOUR HEART, AND WITH ALL YOUR SOUL, AND WITH ALL YOUR MIND.'**

Just as one meal a week will not suffice for maintaining a healthy body so neither will the occasional meeting satisfy or strengthen our spirits.

I know the author of this book personally having spent many hours together, not only in person but over the phone. He is a man with a deep understanding and passion for God. The last conversation I had with him he was just completing a prolonged period of fasting. He lives what he preaches. That's the type of man you want to listen to and learn from.

So, find a quiet place and shut the door; then open your heart along with God's Word, and allow the Holy Spirit to teach you **"wonderful things from His law."**

David Ravenhill, *Author*
Surviving the Anointing
Siloam Springs, AR

Introduction

As a baby Christian, I was taught the great value of developing a quiet time with God; or as I came to call it, a date with Jesus!

I used to wonder why it was that people had such inside into the things of God. How is it that some preachers would preach expository messages full of information and history, but my heart didn't seem to be engaged; and then there were those preachers who said very little but made my heart burn with holy fire. I'm sure you have experienced this.

It didn't take me long to discover and understand why God used some of these servants so mightily. They had discovered the power of God in the secret place of prayer; in being alone with God for hours at a time.

What is a Quiet Time?

A quiet time is a time that is set aside to meet Jesus in the secret place of prayer; yes, it is the place where the Bible can be read, notes of what God is presently saying to our heart is written on a journal and then be presented with the challenge on how to walk out the newfound truth. This is to be done daily.

I asked my mentor at that time, "Do I have to do this every day?" His response changed my life and said, "How much do you love Jesus? And why would you not want to see His lovely face daily?" That settled it for me.

For starters, a quiet time should be done daily – we must fan the flame daily lest it dies. A consistent quiet time is the key the unlocks many things for us. My pastor used to tell me, "If you don't pray one day, it will eventually catch up with you! You may not see the consequence on Monday or Tuesday or the next day, but you will eventually pay for is someday!"

The practice of fasting and holding night watches came a little later as my heart became more acquainted with the sweet presence of my King and my longing to see Him grew.

Life Begins Within

After putting to practice these blessed spiritual exercises, I began to experience a whole life transformation. I can honestly attribute my spiritual vision, passion, perseverance, and zeal for God to these powerful exercises.

During this time, Psalm 42:1 became very real to me: "As the deer pants [longingly] for the water brooks, So my soul pants [longingly] for You, O God." (Psalm 42:1 Amplified Version)

One thing was true, the more I practiced my quiet times, the hungrier I became for the things of God, then it happened…

The Call

My call to serve Christ with my whole life came to pass. It almost seems that God was testing my devotion towards Him before revealing Himself to me in true fashion. I didn't go looking for any call to the work of ministry. What I did go looking for, was for more of Jesus in my life!

I do believe that quiet times are like a preparation of the soil before seeds can be planted on a field. When the ground is ready according to God's plan, the seeds of God will be planted in it.

My passion to know Christ and to make Him known everywhere I went became a normal way of living. I am still in the race today and I am hungrier now than ever before in my life. I'm still holding dates with Jesus daily, and I just keep falling in love with Him over and over and over again!

Since God has deposited into my heart this knowledge of having and developing a quiet time, I have made it a daily goal of mine to keep it going till the day Jesus takes me home.

My Passion in Writing this Manuscript

My motivation for putting these notes together was birthed in my spirit a few years back. My goal is to bring the hungry servant of Jesus to a higher ground in God; to go after God's heart with a burning zeal; to live a life that will be well-lived and empowered by God's presence.

To all those who pick this book to read, remember the words of our Master when He said, "But seek first the kingdom of God and His righteousness, and all these things shall be added to you." (Matthew 6:33)

If there is anything that we have come to know in God, is that He is a God of order. Everything God does He does in a specific order that pleases Him. He must always be first in our lives if we are to learn His ways. Our lives must be always clothed in humility. We must always take the posture of God needs to be first in everything: this includes every thought and every decision, etc.

As we get ready to dive into this manuscript, please understand my heart in this matter: I have discovered that quiet times with Jesus is the fountain to know the heart of God's thoughts and emotions. It is in the secret place of the Highest, that His secrets are revealed.

As the great A.W. Tozer entitled one of his wonderful books, God Tells the Man Who Cares: God Speaks to Those Who Take Time to Listen, it should be our desire to position to know God's heart.

Apparently, there is something brewing in your spirit along the lines of knowing God more intimately and I'm guessing that this is the reason you picked up this book.

I sincerely pray that your heart will be filled and that you will discover the great mysteries that God has reserved for you.

I may not understand the whole idea behind of what I have written, but one thing I have discovered: all my godly dreams, godly ambitions, all that I ever hope to be – all these plans, are all wrapped-up in having daily quiet times with Jesus!

I challenge you to sit at His feet and learn His ways (Luke 10:39).

-David Mayorga, *Author*

Chapter 1

The Need for Personal Discipline

"In going from point A to point B, though it may appear easy to do - it is not! There is a bridge between the two points called discipline. Way too many people don't like to get on it much less cross it!" Consequently, they never enjoy the blessing that point B brings."
                              - David Mayorga

"Most people want to avoid pain, and discipline is usually painful." - John C. Maxwell

"The discipline of writing something down is the first step toward making it happen."
- Lee Iacocca

"We must all suffer one of two things: the pain of discipline or the pain of regret or disappointment."
                              – Jim Rohn

When we deal with the word discipline in any forum, people quickly cringe at the sound of the word. Not all but way too many people do! Discipline is that one thing that makes people great if they follow through. Discipline is a great rewarder to those who are led by it. So . . .

What is discipline? Let's look at this - Longman's Dictionary has it defined this way: the ability to control your own behavior, so that you do what you are expected to do; also, a way of training your mind or learning to control your behavior.

The definition is clear, discipline is bringing your behavior under submission, so that it may do what it is supposed to do in you.

Early Days of Discipline

As a young man, I can still remember my grandfather getting me up very early on Saturday mornings to go work with him. He would schedule in a lawn that needed to be mowed, or he would take me with him, to sell produce at the local grocery store.

My complaint was always the same, "I'm in school all week; I just want to stay in and watch cartoons!" He would then answer me, "You said you wanted or needed new tennis shoes, didn't you? How do you think you are going to get them? You will have to work for them!" That would settle my argument of going to work every single time.

My early childhood trainings in discipline didn't end there, no sir. As I got into High School, I joined the men's basketball team. Being that my situation was not as easy as I would have loved it to be, I had to get to practice early in the morning. For this, I would jog from home (a little over two miles in distance) daily; and then in the evening I was privileged to do it all over again - run, jog or walk back home!

If I wanted to play in the team, I had to get there. No whining, no crying, and no excuses. As the late Jim Rohn would say, "Don't wish for things to be easier – wish to be better!" Thank God for these early challenges.

I want to tell you that all this unnoticed and unrecognized discipline at that specific time in my life, helped me develop my skills in all areas, not to mention my instinct for the game. I graduated being the Most Valuable Player for my team in my Senior year.

One Thing Leads to Another!

It seemed that my earlier experiences with my grandfather and going to work early on Saturday mornings, prepared me for what awaited me during those high school years. No one knew I did this. I just kept doing it until later in life where

I was able to get a car to drive to school. It was a '67 Ford Mustang, but hey, it was a car that turned on and took me back and forth to school and later to work.

One thing I learned about being disciplined and still to date impacts me, is this: every challenge of discipline that you face, will only prepare you for the next challenge. It will take discipline to get to the other side no matter what! Discipline today, tomorrow, and always.

During my high school years, I also held a job after basketball practice. I worked at a burger place and my boss was also a disciplinarian. My good fortune! He taught me to work hard and be responsible. He taught me to be aware of my sur-roundings and to be creative and productive. He also taught me to not waste my time and be idle. If I had a list of top 10 mentors, he would be in it!

By the time I left that burger place, I was in training to be a team leader. Allow me to say it again: Discipline pays off!

I had been married for a couple of months when I got a job at a manufacturing company. I worked several years under a woman who was a total disciplinarian with vision. She was a no-nonsense type of leader. She didn't mess around. She expected much and so daily, it was a challenge to work for this lady who was my immediate supervisor. Same principles of success were expected, and same order of discipline had to be applied.

I left that workplace to join full-time ministry after about 5 years. Discipline had also paid off there as I was being trained to a supervisor position.

Is There a Reason Why God Comes Calling?

It was shortly after this transition, that God allowed me to pastor a small group of people at a small church in a neighboring city. It was my first full-time ministry opportunity, and definitely the biggest challenge yet. It was God's faithfulness then that kept us, and it is God's faithfulness today that continue to keep us.

I am convinced that if a man or a woman of God can't learn discipline, they will have the hardest time navigating through life, a job, a career, a vocation, a ministry, or any endeavor they want to accomplish.

Having great ideas is only the beginning of an endeavor, but how to get to the finish line of that endeavor is the biggest challenge of them all. You see, people desire greatness, but the price to pay is extremely high. Too many have dreamed big but have failed miserably! Why? It wasn't because of lack of knowledge, skill, and even resources; it was because they had no discipline!

The points I lay out in this book have to do with a disciplined lifestyle. If a person can't keep the promises that he makes to himself, he will never reach his vision, his dreams, and/or his purpose in God.

As you meditate on the chapters of this manuscript, know that every discipline must be committed to if you want to see results. The chapter titles sound exciting and doable; but to walk them out, is not as easy as you might think.

I heard the servant of the Lord Leonard Ravenhill once say, "An experience with God that doesn't cost nothing – does nothing!"

Let it cost you – everything!

Chapter 2

The Discipline of Personal Prayer

"And He came to the disciples and found them sleeping, and He said to Peter, What! Are you so utterly unable to stay awake and keep watch with Me for one hour? All of you must keep awake (give strict attention, be cautious and active) and watch and pray, that you may not come into temptation. The spirit indeed is willing, but the flesh is weak." (Matthew 26:40-41)

When it comes to personal prayer, the subject just seems to be a good idea, but too few apply this spiritual exercise in their own lives. If you have ever wondered why so few people spend quality time with God, the answer is simply this: It is not easy! I'm almost sure that if it was easy, everyone would be doing it!

In putting to practice personal prayer, there always seems to arise an enemy against the practice of it - our very flesh! The flesh has a mind of its own and will not submit to what God desires for it is contrary. Jesus said, **"The Spirit indeed is willing, but the flesh is weak."**

Apart from the flesh being weak, what is the real reason that personal prayer is a real battle.

If you notice when people come to worship God, most people have no trouble in singing songs to the Lord, serving Jesus as ushers or being part of the worship team, etc., or even putting a tithe or giving an offering when the time to give arises. All these things don't require any spiritual effort to attain.

People are very talented, and they can sing as good as any celebrity out there; others are well to do with their careers and can afford to give a great offering to the Lord; but all these are only external merits. It doesn't cost anything to do this, not really.

Now, if we want to deal with the spiritual man, then it gets extremely expensive and suddenly not too many want to pay the price to attain a greater revelation of who Jesus is! Personal prayer is the Cinderella of Christianity – nobody wants her! But for those who are longing to enter into a deeper life in God, personal prayer is perhaps one of the most powerful spiritual exercises to take us there!

Why Is There Such a Battle?

In my opinion, personal prayer is the most powerful weapon in the eyes of the devil. He can't stand a person who prays;

I'm referring to that individual who spends quality time in God's presence. That man or woman who allows themselves to be transfigured by God's glory in the secret place.

In case you are wondering what constitutes quality time in the secret place of prayer, let me share with you what I believe this secret place is:

1. It's the place where the servant of God humbles himself in God's presence with no audience to applaud him.

2. It is the place where a man can pour out his deepest secrets to God and be transparent at the highest level in the face of a loving Father.

3. It is the place where the flesh dies and loses its hold on that man of woman of God.

4. True prayer is not 15 minutes long! Save this for when we are having lunch and praying over our lunch meal. A man should at least consecrate 1 to 2 hours a day in secret prayer.

5. To the degree that you fall in love with Christ, it is to the degree that you make room for time

with God. The more you love Him, the more you seek Him. The rule for personal prayer is solely based on how much we love Him!

You must know that there are people who pray at prayer meetings and special events; then there are man and woman of prayer who spend time with God. I want to be known as a man of prayer! A man who can bow before God in prayer daily, can stand in the presence of any man anytime!

In Developing Quality Time with God!

Let me teach you a few things I have picked up during my walk with Christ when it comes to personal prayer. I have personally used this method and still do as I journey with God in my life and ministry.

I make my life of prayer very simple by applying a few elements to my prayers. These elements keep me focus and flowing in my time alone with God. Here they are:

1. Time for Worship. I spend time in worship as soon as I get on my face before Him. I tell Jesus how much I love Him and what He means to me. I open my heart to His heart in adoration. I can spend a full two hours doing this or more; or I can

spend as little as 15 minutes in worship. You be the judge of your time.

2. Time for Thanksgiving. Giving the Lord thanks and acknowledging Him as the Giver of all the things that I possess is a powerful time to magnify His Name. Giving thanks to God for life, provision, work, opportunities, health, and multiple blessings and so much more should always be offered to Him.

3. Time for Confession. A time to sit quietly with God and confess struggles with sin, compromise, spiritual battles, and wrongs done to others, or any type of unforgiveness – must be addressed daily unto Him. The more specific that you can be in your confession before God, the quicker you will be free from guilt and shame.

4. Time for Intercession. This is a time where one can pray for others. Praying for friends, enemies, saved people or unsaved, should always be done. I believe intercessory prayer is the highest form of prayer. Making a list of names of people that you desire to pray for should be made. Pray for 3 to 5 of those people on the list daily. When

you finish your list, start at the top again. A thing to note is this: When you pray for someone, the Lord may reveal to you some insight into their lives. Feel free to share this "word" with them as the Lord leads you in His time and in His way.

5. Time for Petition. This is the time when we can bring our personal needs before God. Sometimes we need direction, sometimes we need leadership, sometimes we need material things to make it through the week; whatever the need may be, bring it before the Lord. He wants to know about it!

6. Time to Listen. Finally, I always include a time to listen to God. This is a time where you say nothing. You stay quiet before Him. You can be silent waiting for Him to speak to you "a word" or give you guidance. Learn to be silent before Him. This sounds easy but it is not. Try it.

Now that I have laid out a simple method to pray in your personal time, let's get to it. Make every effort to do this daily and consistently around the same time. Another note is that you should make every effort to get in all 6 methods daily in your time with God. You can pray as much as you like and as time will allow you; only remember, your degree of love for Him will always guide you in your secret prayer time.

Chapter 3

The Discipline of Bible Reading!

"BLESSED (HAPPY, fortunate, to be envied) **are the unde-filed** (the upright, truly sincere, and blameless) **in the way** [of the revealed will of God]**, who walk** (order their conduct and conversation) **in the law of the Lord** (the whole of God's revealed will).

2 **Blessed** (happy, fortunate, to be envied) **are they who keep His testimonies, and who seek, inquire for and of Him and crave Him with the whole heart.**

3 **Yes, they do no unrighteousness** [no willful wandering from His precepts]**; they walk in His ways.**

4 **You have commanded us to keep Your precepts, that we should observe them diligently.**

5 **Oh, that my ways were directed and established to ob-serve Your statutes** [hearing, receiving, loving, and obeying them]**!**

6 **Then shall I not be put to shame** [by failing to inherit Your promises] **when I have respect to all Your command-ments.**

7 **I will praise and give thanks to You with uprightness of heart when I learn** [by sanctified experiences] **Your righ-teous judgments** [Your decisions against and punishments for particular lines of thought and conduct].

8 I will keep Your statutes; O forsake me not utterly.
9 How shall a young man cleanse his way? By taking heed and keeping watch [on himself] according to Your word [conforming his life to it].
10 With my whole heart have I sought You, inquiring for and of You and yearning for You; Oh, let me not wander or step aside [either in ignorance or willfully] from Your commandments.
11 Your word have I laid up in my heart, that I might not sin against You." (Psalm 119:1-11 -Amplified Version)

"For the Word that God speaks is alive and full of power [making it active, operative, energizing, and effective]; it is sharper than any two-edged sword, penetrating to the dividing line of the breath of life (soul) and [the immortal] spirit, and of joints and marrow [of the deepest parts of our nature], exposing and sifting and analyzing and judging the very thoughts and purposes of the heart. And not a creature exists that is concealed from His sight, but all things are open and exposed, naked, and defenseless to the eyes of Him with Whom we have to do." (Hebrews 4:12, 13 - Amplified Version)

"Every Scripture is God-breathed (given by His inspiration) and profitable for instruction, for reproof and conviction of sin, for correction of error and discipline in obedience, [and] for training in righteousness (in holy living, in conformity to God's will in thought, purpose, and action), So that the man of God may be complete and proficient, well fitted and thoroughly equipped for every good work." (2 Timothy 3:16, 17 - Amplified Version)

God's Manual for Life!

In the Amplified Version Bible, verse 2 reads like this: **"Bless-ed** (happy, fortunate, to be envied) **are they who keep His testimonies, and who seek, inquire for and of Him and crave Him with the whole heart."**

When a man or woman of God is truly touched by the Spirit of God, a craving to know Christ is manifested. A devotion for the knowledge of God through prayer and Bible intake takes on a whole new meaning.

I have seen freshly born-again believers be set on fire by the Spirit of God and a deep longing and groaning for more of Jesus takes over their lives. Why does this happen in some and not in others is beyond me. All I know is that when a man is touched by God, their lives are altered in a truly amazing way. So, keep the craving for more of Jesus going!

The Penetrating Power of God's Word

I have dedicated this chapter to those who crave for God and His word. One thing is for certain, without God's word, a servant of God will not be able to stand in this wicked world.

The servant of God who has positioned himself to learn God's ways, will discover what God thinks and what God desires of him. It is in the actual discipline of study and meditation that these unveilings of truth come. If one desires to know God in His Word, he will without doubt find God.

If you are ready to read His word and have placed yourself with all your heart at the will of God to learn His ways, then let me share with you some insights that I have discovered as you open your heart to God's revealed Word.

The Spirit of the Word

One of the things that I was thought as a young disciple of Jesus, was to always be led by the Spirit of God in my Bible reading.

First, one must know what the Spirit was saying to the writer. What was God's intent in speaking to the author? What was the writer attempting to convey to his listeners? Was it an exhortation, a warning, was he commending them, was he praising them, or perhaps rebuking or correcting them.

We must first know what the writer is saying to the original audience.

Secondly, we must ask God how these words apply to me as an individual? What is God saying to me personally through the author in what I am reading?

As we ask ourselves, What is God saying to me? – We must have a spirit of humility and willingness to listen to the words we are reading as directives from God for our lives. As we open our spirit to God's spirit, we will hear His voice and be able to allow these holy deposits in us.

I Shall Be Changed!

Transformation begins in me when I allow the Spirit of His word and its original intent to download upon me His glorious revelatory truth.

In Hebrews 4:12, the Scripture says the following: **"For the Word that God speaks is alive and full of power** [making it active, operative, energizing, and effective]; **it is sharper than any two-edged sword, penetrating to the dividing line of the breath of life** (soul) **and** [the immortal] **spirit, and of joints and marrow** [of the deepest parts of our nature], **exposing and sifting and analyzing and judging** the very thoughts and purposes of the heart. And not a creature exists that is concealed from His sight, but all things are open and exposed, naked, and defenseless to the eyes of Him with Whom we have to do."

Let me share with you my mindset and method as I meditate through His Word:

1. I must acknowledge that His Word is alive and full of power.

2. His Word is sharper than any two-edged sword, and it penetrates and divides my soul and my spirit.

3. His Word exposes, sifts, analyzes, and judges my thoughts and intentions of my own heart.

4. When I am in meditation in His Word, I am completely exposed and defenseless to His eyes.

Honoring and Respecting God's Word

Every Scripture is God-breathed (given by His inspiration) and profitable for instruction, for reproof and conviction of sin, for correction of error and discipline in obedience, [and] for training in righteousness (in holy living, in conformity to

God's will in thought, purpose, and action), So that the man of God may be complete and proficient, well fitted and thoroughly equipped for every good work." (2 Timothy 3:16, 17)

Do I believe that God's Word is God's revealed mind? Absolutely. Is there any higher authority than God's Word? Absolutely not! The servant of Jesus must put all His whole being under the direction of this life manual and allow himself to be led by it.

When in debate about matters concerning God: God is always right; man is always wrong.

Whatever God wanted to reveal to man, He did in His Word. Whatever God did not want to reveal to man, He didn't! That settles it for me.

Being that the Scripture is God-breathed, we should lend an open heart and mind to it.

As one opens it to receive from God, please realize that His words are ready to come out of the pages into your very heart. So, the Lord begins to:

1. Give instruction. He desires you and I to know His ways, His thoughts, His intentions – this

includes every area of our lives. I know that we as human beings are very intelligent. We are saturated with information from all the corners of the world. The only thing is that we don't know what we don't know. Or perhaps we don't know how we should know or what we should know! That is why God speaks to our spirit, which in turn, influences our whole being.

2. For reproof and correction of sin. The Word of God sometimes corrects us in our wayward ways. It brings us back to the center of God's will. God won't allow us to keep going off the path for long. He will come in and bring reproof to our way of thinking which is affecting our lifestyle. Always remember, God's way are different than ours!

3. For training in righteousness. Also, God's word will not only correct us, but will present the right actions to take, so we can make the necessary changes that will please God. We must live to please Him and Him alone.

4. So that we may be complete. It is God's desire to bring completeness to the man of God by educating him in God's ways and purpose. It is

only when the man of God is walking and living in the center of God's will, that God is honored by him.

Different Methods of Reading

There are many books written regarding different ways of reading and studying the Bible. Many have study methods that focus on history, others study characters of the Bible, others love to study the poetic side of the Scriptures, and others are into the study of prophecy and eschatological perspectives. Whether you like one style over the other, I leave that up to you the reader.

I will say that I have discovered a method that better suits my desire and pursuit after God's heart, and that method is to read my bible in deep meditation. Don't get me wrong – I love to study my Bible in all the areas I mentioned, but deep meditation is my favorite.

In deep meditation, I personally use a Read the Bible in a Year outline. I have for most of my Christian walk. This keeps me flowing daily in my quiet times. I only read small portions daily and this is done on purpose. You see, I used to read the whole Bible at least 3 times a year at one point; then my hunger for the things of the Spirit grew. I now read my Bible once every 3 years. I enjoy basking and soaking into His presence when I read. This is how God and I have this awesome love relationship!

It is my sincere prayer that you develop your own love-relationship with Jesus. Stay hungry for more of Him.

Chapter 4

The Discipline of Journaling!

"He also taught me, and said to me:
"Let your heart retain my words;
Keep my commands, and live.
Get wisdom! Get understanding!
Do not forget, nor turn away from the words of my mouth.
Do not forsake her, and she will preserve you;
Love her, and she will keep you.
Wisdom is the principal thing;
Therefore, get wisdom.
And in all your getting, get understanding." (Proverbs 4:4-7)

"Write the vision
And make it plain on tablets,
That he may run who reads it." (Habakkuk 2:2)

"This will be written for the generation to come,
That a people yet to be created may praise the LORD."
(Psalm 102:18)

Why Keep a Journal?

When reading God's word, depending on your desire to understand and the willingness of your heart to be taught, you will receive a lot of wisdom for your daily life.

When pondering or meditating verses in the Scriptures, truth will come out of those verses, and you don't want to miss all that God is presently speaking to you. You will want to make note of it and write it down.

Yes, these notes have so much power to transform your heart and mind, that you will want to write them and pay attention to their instruction.

As you allow these present-day truths to enter your heart and mind and then flow through your hands as you write, a deep mystical work will take effect in you. You will then be reminded constantly of what was written. I do believe the Holy Spirit will use all you have written to start a transformational process.

Different Journals for Different People

Journaling has been taken to mean different things to different people.

For some, journaling means to write down prayers. For others, it means to write down prayer requests or make note of answered prayers. I have seen others make journals of their encounters with God or keep a daily diary of events as they walk with God. A friend of mine used to keep a journal of all the things he was grateful for as the Lord kept blessing his life.

The Art of Writing

I believe that creative writing is art. In writing down thoughts that come from the heart, an expression is released into the world. To me, art, is an expression of what the heart sees. Years ago, I read an article that praised the value found in writing or journaling. This article alluded to the fact that any type of art, has the effect of slowing us down enough that we are then able to hear our inner being. This experience in turn, helps us reflect, contemplate, or helps us digest the wisdom that we are jotting down.

When we become intentional about our writing, we then become alert to all that we are putting down on paper. I have noticed that handwritten notes are more powerful than typing on a typewriter or computer. For some reason, what is written makes a more deliberate impact on the mind and heart. Maybe it's just me, but it has kept me going for all these 35-plus years.

My Journaling Style

In writing my journal, I have developed a habit of putting a title and a date to my daily entries. This always helps me when I refer to it. Why would I want to refer to it? Well, there are times when spiritual dryness hits or discouragement comes like a flood into my life; it is in times like these, that the Spirit of God will remind me of something I have read, meditated, or studied in put in my journal. It is truly beneficial for the long haul in spiritual matters.

One of the things I have learned in life up to now is this: If you are making plans to live a life that makes an impact in some way, you want to pay attention to detail. Every little thing you do, will pay big dividends in the end. Every little effort you make (whether acknowledged by someone or not,) will pay you back in a great way later in life! As the Scripture has taught us in the law of sowing and reaping, it applies to everything in our lives! Sow great stuff in the present, so you can reap great stuff in the future! This is a daily discipline.

Leaving a Legacy!

In closing this chapter, let me add a note that has been close to my heart.

When I came into the kingdom of God, I must admit, I didn't like to read and the thought of writing anything on paper, had never entered my mind since writing essays in high school.

I'm not sure when exactly, but something happened in me...

A desire to read started to move my heart and begin to buy books at thrift stores, garage sales, and at the local Christian bookstore. I would buy a book here and there and my love for reading began as I pursued God's heart.

I always read with the author in mind. I would ask myself questions like: "Why did the author say this? Or "How does He know Christ so well?" In reading biographies or autobiographies, I started to ask serious questions like, "Why did they leave everything to follow God to the darkest place in India, Africa, South America, etc.?"

The thought that they would leave everything behind to follow Jesus where He would lead, and write it down on a book, impacted me so profoundly! Leaving notes written in book form or in journal form, impacted my life in a very deep way and then I understood the power of the written word.

I started to write down my thoughts and God's thoughts on paper after that. People would ask me, "Why are you writing notes down?" I would only respond and say, "I am leaving a legacy for someone else!"

It might be that your children or your children's children might never be the same because of your personal journal in the mysteries of God! Have you seriously thought about it?

My desire to write and journal my sincere thoughts of God and what He was saying to me personally, was birthed in me, because someone else did it with me in mind. It is my prayer: **"Yes, even when I am old and gray-headed, O God, for-sake me not,** [but keep me alive] **until I have declared Your mighty strength to** [this] **generation, and Your might and power to all that are to come."** (Psalm 71:18 -Amplified Version)

Chapter 5

The Discipline of Fasting!

"Then Jesus was led up by the Spirit into the wilderness to be tempted by the devil. And when He had fasted forty days and forty nights, afterward He was hungry." (Matthew 4:1)

First Things First

Fasting is a temporary act of self-denial. By going without food for a brief period, we become more aware of our need for daily sustenance. Fasting seems to slow life down so that we become more conscious of God and how He moves in our midst and works His wonders.

During these times of fasting, we focus our attention on God, and all that He has in store for us. Fasting has a way of making us more receptive to the things of the Spirit and teaches us about us. Nothing exposes our true self than a good fast!

Once we see ourselves as we really are, true humility will be birthed in us. It is this humility that brings about true repentance. Once we repent, the river of God's power will begin to flow once again through our lives. It is at this place where we realize that living our life for God's honor and glory, is what life is all about!

Twisting God's Arm through Fasting!

I have heard people teach about fasting through my Christian life. I have heard some preachers and teachers say that fasting is a good way to get what you want. In other words, fast so you can twist God's arm, per se. God will see your sacrifice and give you what you are asking for. This might be or not be.

One thing I have learned in my research and practice of fasting, is that God is more interested in having all of me than me getting my "list of toys."

Anyone who has been walking with God for a good amount of time, knows that the biggest enemy we face is our selfishness. Nothing is more powerful than when self is in control. Through self, we hinder God. Through self, we miss out on God's will. Yes, it is through self that miracles, signs, and wonders, will not be seen in our lives!

How to Overcome Self!

I have heard believers say, "I want to fast so I can lose weight."

Others say, "I am fasting so I can get the car I want or need." Others are more spiritual and say, "I want to fast so I can see revival and so my church can grow!"

Though God may answer our sincere wishes through fasting, let me say that we are missing the point of fasting.

I am a simple person when it comes to theology and daily disciplines; so, my idea of fasting is a simple one: Fast so you can bring the flesh under subjection and God have His way in you! Stop wishing for external stuff and learn humility and brokenness at all costs. With all thy getting, get broken!

Fasting Removes Unbelief (a fruit of the flesh.)

"Then the disciples came to Jesus privately and said, "Why could we not cast it out?" So, Jesus said to them, "Because of your unbelief; for assuredly, I say to you, if you have faith as a mustard seed, you will say to this mountain, 'Move from here to there,' and it will move; and nothing will be impossible for you. However, this kind does not go out except by prayer and fasting." (Matthew 17:19-21)

When flesh is in control of our lives, we will produce fruit that is displeasing to the Lord. Let me demonstrate: When flesh is leading our lives, we will end up sinning against God. It may sound extreme to you, but I know by experience, that flesh will bring about corruption into your life. It will be painful and degrading, not to mention embarrassing!

When we walk in the flesh, we can only sin! Walking in the flesh makes us powerless in the matters of the Spirit; weak when following Christ's will; and if that is not enough, confused in life without the guidance of God's Spirit which provides leadership for all areas of our life.

In the text above, the disciples came to Christ after being embarrassed by a demonic spirit – they couldn't cast it out from the demon-possessed son. Listen: **"And when they had come to the multitude, a man came to Him, kneeling down to Him and saying, "Lord, have mercy on my son, for he is an epileptic and suffers severely; for he often falls into the fire and often into the water. So, I brought him to Your disciples, but they could not cure him."** (Matthew 17:14-16)

As a response to this, Jesus said, **"O faithless and perverse generation..."** (Matthew 17:17a)

The issue here was faith, or the lack of. Jesus called it out.

The issue that we must learn is the following: the disciples were weak and powerless – it is not that the demon was more powerful than Christ! The disciples were carnal and unbelieving; therefore, there was nothing they could do to cure this demon-possessed boy. Jesus said the real problem here is unbelief! This kind of unbelief only comes out through prayer and fasting.

When self is in control, our lives are powerless to follow God's will.

No Substitutes to Obtain Christ's Power!

Though one may be intellectual, smart, skillful, and charismatic, this doesn't make you a person with spiritual power. As far as the kingdom of God is concerned, that man is spiritually poor and powerless!

Spiritual power can only be found in Christ and in our yielding to His Spirit daily. Living a humble and broken life before God is the key to spiritual power and ascendency [dominion.]

A humble and broken person before God might not appear as much outwardly, but as he starts praying, hell will shake, the demons will tremble and God through intercessory prayer will establish His divine order! Things don't get set in divine order by natural weapons and strategy; the things of God get set in place through intercessory prayer!

Fasting: Why and How.

Let me write this small part of this chapter and share with you my experience in why I fast, and the how I practice my fasting.

The "why" I fast is done with two things in view. The first one is that I fast because I need it. Understanding how my flesh operates in me and how it wants to derail my life from God's will, motivates me go into warfare mode. I fast first and foremost to keep myself in check before God.

Secondly, I fast also as the Holy Spirit leads me to it. There is a sense that I get in my heart and mind to fast. I will then ask the Holy Spirit how long I need to fast. He will always show me, and I just do it.

I make every attempt to be faithful to my fasting times. I take my fasting days seriously and commit myself to it. This must be done if you want to complete the process for as long as it needs to be. It is not easy, but even that, it takes discipline and lots of it.

What Does My Fast Consist Of?

Like I said before, I am simple when it comes to my theology and daily spiritual practices; so, when I fast, I fast. So, twenty-four hours without eating (liquids only) constitutes one day of fasting. If I'm doing 3 days of fasting, this means that I will be not eating anything for 72 hours. It's that simple!

There are so many ways to fast from what I have discovered in my research; but to be honest, knowing what I know about the flesh and how food strengthens it; when fasting, I don't want to eat anything.

So, when I hear that someone wants to do a fast, I encourage them to go without food for the length of the fast. The flesh is very astute and doesn't want to be harnessed or brought into subjection, especially to the Spirit of God. So, the flesh always compromises with us and says, "Just fast till 12pm" or "Do a Daniel Fast." The flesh will do anything to stay alive! Take note of this in your own life.

Finally, if you are under a doctor's care and are taking medication, please consult your physician before you go into any type of fasting. It might be that your immune system will not take the fast well and affect you negatively. I am not a doctor, but I have seen people get ill or have side effects due to extensive fasting or protracted fasting.

Seek to be as spiritual as you can be but be wise as well!

Chapter 6

The Discipline of Walking in Humility & Brokenness!

"Let this same attitude and purpose and [humble] mind be in you which was in Christ Jesus: [Let Him be your example in humility:] Who, although being essentially one with God and in the form of God [possessing the fullness of the attributes which make God God], did not think this equality with God was a thing to be eagerly grasped or retained, But stripped Himself [of all privileges and rightful dignity], so as to assume the guise of a servant (slave), in that He became like men and was born a human being. And after He had appeared in human form, He abased and humbled Himself [still further] and carried His obedience to the extreme of death, even the death of the cross! Therefore [because He stooped so low] God has highly exalted Him and has freely bestowed on Him the name that is above every name, that in (at) the name of Jesus every knee should (must) bow, in heaven and on earth and under the earth, and every tongue [frankly and openly] confess and acknowledge that Jesus Christ is Lord, to the glory of God the Father." (Philippians 2:5-11 – Amplified Version)

In my walk with God, I have come to realize that there is a handful of important elements that make this Christian walk work. Though there are plenty of spiritual exercises that we can put into practice, I don't believe there is a substitute for these two specific elements: humility and brokenness.

I have watched closely through the years how God has chosen some people to serve Him in different levels and have always taken notice of what makes those vessels, (not perfect by any means,) but outstanding, to say the least.

As I would watch and keep my focus on what made these world-changers impactful, I noticed that in the center of their being, they practiced humility and were broken vessels due to their willingness to put God first before their own wants and needs!

Godly Humility

I'm sure I can dive into the Webster's or Oxford's Dictionary for a definition to the word humility; but I believe God gave me a definition more adequate for those who dare to walk with Him. My definition of humility is as simple as 1, 2, 3. Humility simply put means, ***"putting God first in all things."*** This is a better definition than all the ones I have read thus far.

Putting God first in all things is exactly what Jesus did. He put the Father's wishes first; He put the Father's desires first; yes, He put God's plan for humanity first, before His own plan of having (what we would call) a normal life! Jesus Himself said, "For I have come down from heaven, not to do My own will, but the will of Him who sent Me." (John 6:38). Now that is humility in action.

The Discipline of Humility

What is the discipline of humility then? To have a discipline of humility is to live with the consciousness of humility always before you; an alertness of the Holy Spirit's promptings and sensitivity to this state of mind. Always aware that you don't live for yourself but for King Jesus. Are you getting this?

To walk in the discipline of humility is to walk harnessed by the Lord. You are not your own and you walk in this reality. You understand that your life is NOT about you, but about Him and what He has commissioned you to do!

To be able to follow God as He would desire, is for one to do exactly what Jesus did when He came to earth. The Scripture in Philippians says about Christ that He didn't think equality with God. Though He was God, He didn't use His credentials as such! No sir! "[He} **stripped Himself** [of all privileges and rightful dignity,] **so as to assume the guise of a servant** (slave)."

To walk in the discipline of humility means just this: a daily walk of stripping yourself of your privileges and rightful dignity, so as to assume the guise of a slave."

Brokenness!

What is brokenness? *Brokenness* is being so dead to self and so alive to God, that your flesh doesn't have the power or influence to stop you from obeying God, no matter what He is asking of you to do!

Whereas humility is more of an inward heartfelt devotion to put God first; brokenness, is the action taken by the wishful desire of the Holy Spirit wanting to release Himself through the human vessel.

With my heart and my mind, I tell God, "Whatever you want me to do Jesus, I will do!" Even so, it is with my actions, when God says to me, "Ok David. I want you to do this for Me!" And I obey Him without delay. This would be brokenness in action. Releasing the desire of the Holy Spirit through my life is *brokenness!*

The Discipline of Brokenness

The discipline of *brokenness* can be better illustrated by the story of the woman with the alabaster flask of costly perfume. Listen to this: **"And while He was in Bethany,** [a guest] **in the house of Simon the leper, as He was reclining** [at table]**, a woman came with an alabaster jar of ointment** (perfume) **of pure nard, very costly and precious; and she broke the jar and poured** [the perfume] **over His head. But there were some who were moved with indignation and said to themselves, to what purpose was the ointment** (perfume) **thus wasted?"** (Mark 14:3, 4)

Walking in the discipline of *brokenness* has several characteristics to it. A few of them can be learned here in this story. The woman came over to where Jesus was sitting and proceeded to anoint Him breaking an alabaster jar of costly and precious perfume.

Brokenness is willing to break the desires of the flesh to please God. When an individual is walking in *brokenness*, they are willing to do anything to please God. Anything that dares to get in the way, you can be sure, they will break it or shred it to pieces! All for the sake of Christ. They see the need to release every drop of costly perfume on the body of Christ! This is the mindset of those who walk in *brokenness*.

Secondly, a person walking in *brokenness*, will never put value on the external box or flask, but on what is inside of it. In this case, the costly precious oil was the thing of value. This symbolizes the Holy Spirit's desires and wishes. These are always more valuable than anything this world can afford!

Finally, those servants who walk in *brokenness* don't care about who is watching, whether there are people or no people. They only do things for the audience of One – for Jesus only! Criticism, fear, doubt, unbelief, or personal preferences hold no right on these broken vessels; yes, these who have been crucified by Christ and no longer live for themselves!

To live in the discipline of *brokenness*, one must understand the Apostle Paul's mindset to its very core, when he said, **"and He died for all, that those who live should live no longer for themselves, but for Him who died for them and rose again."** (2 Corinthians 5:15). It's time to enter in!

Chapter 7

The Discipline of Waiting!

"Impatience is the fruit of immaturity."
                                        -Author Unknown

"Wait on the LORD;
Be of good courage,
And He shall strengthen your heart;
Wait, I say, on the LORD!"
(Psalm 27:14)

Waiting on anything is never a joyful time for anyone. When you ask any individual if they like to wait – almost all of them will tell you how much they hate to wait on anything.

People don't like to wait for test results, medical diagnoses, wait at the grocery line, at bank line, at a drive-thru window, etc. It is obvious that waiting is not anyone's favorite experience. Yet, in the Lord, waiting, seems to be a key component in the lives of those who are chosen by Him.

If I would have to take a safe guess, God chooses people who have learned the discipline of waiting for special tasks. I know that waiting on the Lord sounds like a neat thing to do, but to be honest, everyone really hates doing it. We all we want answers and results now; not later, and most definitely not tomorrow or next week or next month!

Waiting is one of those things that works in an individual's character. It is such a tool in developing a person in the inward parts of his or her life, that to bypass it, or neglect it, would seem wrong. Waiting is a tool that God uses to exercise our resolve and devotion to Jesus, our Lord.

Once God sees that we can handle the discipline of waiting, He will commission us accordingly, but not before! Through small, insignificant tests, God will work in us. Every test doing its perfect work in us, increasing in intensity every single time, until the Lord renders us ready for the task He has for us.

I want to show us how this discipline of waiting plays a huge role in our life, work, career and ministry before God.

Moses, the Meek Servant

"Now the man Moses was very meek (gentle, kind, and humble) or above all the men on the face of the earth." (Numbers 12:3)

Moses was not always meek; Moses was not always kind and gentle, not to mention humble. Moses at one time, was the opposite of this. He was impatient and harsh. He was not a very temperate man at one time. But God worked on him throughout his life.

Now, God had some plans and Moses would be the one to hear those plans and see them with his own eyes. So it came to pass that the Lord wanted to meet with Moses up on Mount Sinai. Listen to what the Word of God says: **"The Lord said to Moses, "Come up to me on the mountain. Stay there, and I will give you the stone tablets with the teachings and the commandments I have written for the people's instruction." Moses set out with his assistant Joshua, and Moses went up on the mountain of God. He said to the leaders, "Wait here for us until we come back to you. Aaron and Hur are here with you. Take all your disagreements to them." So, Moses went up on the mountain, and the cloud covered it. The glory of the Lord settled on Mount Sinai. For six days the cloud covered it, and on the seventh day the Lord called to Moses from inside the cloud. To the Israelites, the glory of the Lord looked like a raging fire on top of the mountain. Moses entered the cloud as he went up the mountain. He stayed on the mountain 40 days and 40 nights."** (Exodus 24:12-18)

The Scripture says that God called Moses to climb the mountain because He wanted to give him the stone tablets with teachings and commandments. After climbing the mountain, nothing really happened up on the mountain for nearly 6 days. The only thing Moses could see was a cloud cover!

Allowing Impatience to Rule!

One thing I have noticed about some believers is that who have a calm-natured demeanor don't really struggle with impatience as much as those who have a mindset with zeal and vision to conquer the world.

When we don't allow our sin-nature to come under the Lordship of Christ, to come to the cross of Christ and die, we will turn into a walking time bomb. Under the right circumstances and at the right time, we will go off the deep-end and allow our flesh to create something due to our impatience. Our flesh only knows to sin! It will always breed corruption and destruction. So waiting is key if we are to see the hand of God move in godly fashion. Waiting is definitely not for the weak-hearted!

Can you imagine Moses dealing with his impatience at this very moment? I can almost see this scenario: Moses could have lost it and said, "I'm going home; forget this nonsense!

What kind of joke is God playing on me? Where is He anyways? As the hours passed, the impatience grew! Most of us what have gone home by now but not Moses – then the Word of God says, **"and on the seventh day the Lord called Moses from inside the cloud."**

You see, the discipline of waiting had paid off for Moses. He was no at a divine place where he could now be a recipient of God's revelation. This is what we are aiming for.

Don't let your impatience steal anything from you any longer.

Chapter 8

The Discipline of Obedience!

When it comes to obedience, it is not as easy as it may seem; obedience requires action. If one doesn't move to the march of the drummer, one may stay behind and be out of sync. Obedience is and will always entail action!

Obedience is the word that makes things come to fruition. God can have an excellent idea, plan, or strategy; but if we don't have the faith to believe what He is telling us, we won't obey Him. We won't see or experience what God wants to do in us and through us!

Let me break down this word obedience just for the sake of study. Obedience in Oxford's Dictionary has it as *compliance with an order, request, or law or submission to another's authority.* In simple terms, this would mean that whoever has authority over you, might request from you to do something. If you do what you are asked, you will be walking in obedience.

When we deal with obedience from a total secular perspective, it means to comply or be in submission to another's authority. But when you add the Jesus factor to it, if you will, it changes it from a mere request, to a passionate pursue to please God. You may not see it as such, but if you allow me, let me show you what this mindset is all about.

Function as a Slave of Jesus!

I know that the word slave could be a bad word in a sense and when you add the word Jesus Christ to the equation, it almost makes its use contradictory. Someone may say, "How can you talk about slavery or being a slave to anything when Christ has made us free?" Very good point.

Now, allow me to make my point clear as I introduce this new man made in the image of Christ – a slave for Jesus! This is the type of man that God called us to be when He saved us and transferred us over to His kingdom.

You see my friend; you and I were in bondage to the enemy. The flesh, the devil, the world – all these tyrants controlled us. We were slaves to these wicked elements. We, by our own desire, were held captive to these things until Christ came to set us free!

Now, Christ's freedom came to us at the perfect time that we may be free from these tyrants; in return, we would become His bondservants (His slaves, if you will). We were bought with price – an expensive one at that! So, we have been freed from sin that we may be slaves to Christ. The Apostle Paul laid it out this way: **"Paul, a slave of Christ Jesus, called to be an apostle, set apart for the gospel of God..."** (Romans 1:1 – The Lexham English Bible)

It is my belief that to be an effective slave, one must learn obedience to their Master. In our case as believers, Christ is not our "buddy," He is our Lord and King and Master! He calls the shots! My job is only to obey the Lamb of God wherever He may lead!

With this said, my prayer is that our obedience may take on a whole new understanding. Serving Christ is a life of total obedience. Half-hearted devotion has no place in God's kingdom. Serving our King and Master is not for the weak, shy, and timid. It is a call to abandonment from all earthliness. A cry to undo all the strings that may tie us down to our lower nature.

We don't become obedient to the Lord Jesus because we "have to"; we become obedient to Jesus our Master because we "get to!"

The Discipline of Obedience
In the discipline of obedience, we learn to live it by being

conscious at every turn in our lives. Every decision, every thought, every word we hear and every word we speak, not to mention the actions we will be taking – all these must be harnessed and brought under the Lordship of Christ in obedience to His voice. It must be our desire to honor Jesus by keeping all His wishes.

Marching to the beat of His drum, is the call of every true servant of Jesus!

Quick to Hear; Quick to Obey!

My mentor used to always tell me, "When God calls you to do something for Him and you know very well that He is asking you to obey – be quick to hear Him and quick to obey Him!"

A servant of Jesus who still doubts and plays games with God, will always be in the middle of the fence with his emotions, his decisions, his will, his own agenda, enslaved by his own ambitions, plans, goals and ideas.

This man or woman of God will all through their Christian walk, be doubters at best, and consequently, their lives will be unproductive for God. Listen to the wisdom of the Apostle James as he puts it so well in his letter: **"...for he who doubts is like a wave of the sea driven and tossed by the** wind. **For let not that man suppose that he will receive anything from the Lord; he is a double-minded man, unstable in all his ways."** (James 1:6-8)

As I close this chapter, please hear my heart in all of this. When Christ died for us, it wasn't just so we could just join a church group and enjoy beautiful services accompanied by great praise and worship music, awesome preaching, and teaching, and have a good old time in God's presence.

When Christ died for us – it was so that we may lend ourselves to Him fully so that He may fill our lives with His glory; then, we were to be light to the world (the lost) and tell them how many great things God has done for us!

To be an expression of God's glory on the earth is the ultimate mandate apart from meeting God daily in the secret place of prayer. As the late servant of God David Wilkerson would passionately say: *"All ministry must be birthed out of intimacy with God!"*

I pray these notes help, in some small way, get us to this place! Blessings.

Chapter 9

The Discipline of Perseverance!

Allow me to share one more chapter in this wonderful pursuit of God. Let me talk to you about perseverance. Perseverance means persistence in doing something despite difficulty or delay in achieving success. This is one of those words that many Christians use in conversation but don't practice. Why don't they practice it? Because it is not easy to do! Others think that perseverance is a "neat and cool" word to use when being around Christian peers; and yet to others, the word perseverance has never entered their minds!

Perseverance is not a word that carnal Christians know anything about; it is more a word tailored for the hungry disciple of Jesus. Like the spiritual man, perseverance is a word that must be spiritually discerned. The flesh wants nothing to do with perseverance!

In seeing deeply what God desires from us; one must like Hannah (1 Samuel 1:10,) pray until our anguish and vehement weeping, reaches His throne. And like the great Apostle John said, **"And if we know that he hears us—whatever we ask—we know that we have what we asked of him."** (1 John 5:15)

Let us learn about this great spiritual discipline of perseverance...

"See how the farmer waits for the precious fruit of the earth, waiting patiently for it until it receives the early and latter rain. You also be patient. Establish your hearts, for the coming of the Lord is at hand." (James 5:7, 8)

Perseverance speaks to us of *time*. To persevere basically means that we must continue to ask for something that was promised. We pray until it manifests!

Now, persevering is most definitely not for the weak in heart!

People who persevere are of a different breed. You may disagree with me on this, but I have lived long enough, and have known God long enough, to know, that unless one is willing to persevere and get what was promised, one will never see the promise in its fullness.

Allow me to share what I believe is to be the heart of God in the issue of waiting for the manifestation of any given promise or prophetic word given.

"I Want it *Now!*"

Believers have a bad habit and it's no different than unbelievers. The habit is that they think life works like a microwave oven. People have the idea that we can turn life on and off by the flick of a switch! Have you noticed this?

The terrible feeling of not fitting into a new shirt or pants, must be one of the greatest disgusting feelings ever. Not being able to lose weight soon enough for the upcoming class reunion; and unable to fit into that suit or that lovely dress for the occasion, is a terrible feeling. I know I am making this more dramatic than what it seems; but you know exactly what I mean.

There are things you can't change overnight; they will take time and discipline to see results.

The Law of Sowing and Reaping!

"Do not be deceived, God is not mocked; for whatever a man sows, that he will also reap." (Galatians 6:7)

The law of sowing and reaping is always present and always at work! We can't do away with it; we can't erase it; we can't ignore it; and we can't deny it! When it comes to the law of sowing and reaping, we are all under its mighty hand!

Yes, we will all be held accountable to it when the results come in; it will all come out in the wash!

Therefore, it would be of great wisdom, to learn its principle and redirect our life by basing our newfound understanding of it. Let us learn what it means and how we can better be led by it.

Enamored with the *Now*!

For some strange reason, believers think that God will give you and I what we want or need now! People come and get prayed for in our meetings in hopes that God will do a special work right now! That is what they say to themselves when they are driving to church: "I want God to do a miracle for me now!" Or "I hope so and so is praying for people, so I can get in on it and receive my miracle!" Etc.

This is the typical cry in people's lives today. They need something and they need it now!

Do I believe God can do a miracle based on people's faith? Absolutely! I believe God can heal or reach anyone at any time. I believe that people in dire need can get an answer immediately or even as they drive to the prayer meeting. I have never doubted God working in this way.

Now, if this is the way that you have chosen to live out your life, then good luck with it. It will soon come to pass where God will have to sit you down and have a serious talk with you regarding your life principles.

It can't be that you live so irresponsibly; and by this, I mean in negligence, in rebellion, and religiously ignorant, under false teachings that move in metaphysical faith and are founded on greed and self; and then expect God to carry you through because of your foolishness! I'm telling you; it will not happen!

Walking in God's Design

When the Lord gives us a word, a prophetic promise, etc., He is waiting for you to do something with it. Let us see...

"And again, He began to teach by the sea. And a great multitude was gathered to Him, so that He got into a boat and sat in it on the sea; and the whole multitude was on the land facing the sea. Then He taught them many things by parables and said to them in His teaching: "Listen! Behold, a Sower went out to sow. And it happened, as he sowed, that some seed fell by the wayside; and the birds of the air came and devoured it. Some fell on stony ground, where it did not have much earth; and immediately it sprang up because it had no depth

of earth. But when the sun was up it was scorched, and because it had no root it withered away. And some seed fell among thorns; and the thorns grew up and choked it, and it yielded no crop. But other seed fell on good ground and yielded a crop that sprang up, increased and produced: some thirtyfold, some sixty, and some a hundred." And He said to them, "He who has ears to hear, let him hear!" And He said to them, "Do you not understand this parable? How then will you understand all the parables? The sower sows the word. And these are the ones by the wayside where the word is sown. When they hear, Satan comes immediately and takes away the word that was sown in their hearts. These likewise are the ones sown on stony ground who, when they hear the word, immediately receive it with gladness; and they have no root in themselves, and so endure only for a time. Afterward, when tribulation or persecution arises for the word's sake, immediately they stumble. Now these are the ones sown among thorns; they are the ones who hear the word, and the cares of this world, the deceitfulness of riches, and the desires for other things entering in choke the word, and it becomes unfruitful. But these are the ones sown on good ground, those who hear the word, accept it, and bear fruit: some thirtyfold, some sixty, and some a hundred." (Mark 4:1-9, 13-21)

The Sower went to sow seed, the Scripture says. This is God Himself sowing His word. Where is He sowing it? He is sowing it on the ground. The Bible teaches us that this Sower sowed seed in four different types of grounds: By the wayside, stony ground, thorny ground, and finally, on good ground.

The ground is the heart of the believer. He will not clean the ground and prepare it; this is the believer's responsibility. It's up to us to make good use of the ground and we must cultivate it, and have it always prepared for when He speaks.

Cultivating the Seed!

In cultivating the seed, one must learn to first always prepare their hearts (the ground) to receive that prophetic word or promise. By the way, you know what kind of ground you have before you!

Once the seed is in the ground, your ground; it is your duty to cultivate it by watering it. You must know that it is your promise; it is your future! You either prepare it or you don't.

After this, you wait and wait and wait, until...until you see the plant coming out of the ground. This takes time in case you didn't realize it. As it grows on a day-to-day basis, you are still called to work it and cultivate it. Don't walk away from it; don't consider it as something worthless – remember, it's your future!

You begin to be more intentional with your little plant knowing that it has a promising effect that favors you. So, you dig around it, you keep the ground clean around it; you will even build a fence around it to protect it. Why? Because it is your future!

Staying focus till the end is not easy. It takes perseverance; it takes discipline!

The Fruit is Here!

Finally, one day, you begin to eat of its fruit. The results will be solely based on your obedience, responsibility, cultivation, perseverance, and discipline!

When you inspect your fruit and see that it is delicious and worthy of sharing with someone else, you will share it with joy! Usually if something doesn't taste good, you won't share it; but if you have done your part in bringing this promise to pass; know that God has done His part!

This is God's design for us who believe!

Chapter 10

Fasting Options & Notes

Fasting Option #1

[ ]   24 hours constitute a day of fasting.

[ ]   Not eating food is fasting.

[ ]   Fast 40 complete days without food, but drink fluids.
        Unless the Lord told you to fast without drinking
        water or fluids, drink as much fluids as needed.

[ ]   Spend daily quality time in prayer and in God's Word.
        Follow some of the principles outlined in this book.
        Also, follow the Prayer and Fasting Guide in chapter
        11 of this book.

[ ]   Don't forget to keep a journal.

Fasting Option #2

[ ]   Fast till 6pm every day for 40 days.

[ ]   Spend daily quality time in prayer and in God's Word.

Follow some of the principles outlined in this book. Also, follow the Prayer and Fasting Guide in chapter 11 of this book.

[ ]   Don't forget to keep a journal.

Fasting Option #3

[ ]   Fasting at Different Times:

> Fast Monday till 12pm.
> Fast Tuesday till 3pm.
> Fast Wednesday till 6pm.
> Fast Thursday till 9pm.
> Fast Friday ALL day!

[ ]   On Saturday you start the process all over again, starting at 12pm.

[ ]   Spend daily quality time in prayer and in God's Word. Follow some of the principles outlined in this book. Also, follow the Prayer and Fasting Guide in chapter 11 of this book.

[ ]   Don't forget to keep journal.

Special Note:

"When we fast, we bring the old man, the flesh, down; when we pray and read God's Word, our spirit rises higher!   If we fast and pray, only God knows the potential of what we can become in His hands!"

- pd

Chapter 11

Prayer & Fasting Guide

AM I IN CHRIST?

Day 1: *Am I in the Faith? Am I Really Born-Again? How Saved Am I?*

Scriptures:

"Test yourselves to see if you are in the faith; examine yourselves! Or do you not recognize this about yourselves, that Jesus Christ is in you—unless indeed you fail the test?" (2 Cor. 13:5)

"For God so loved the world that He gave His only begotten Son, that whoever believes in Him should not perish but have everlasting life." (John 3:16)

A. Evaluate your personal walk with God today. Ask yourself these deep personal questions:

1. Is your heart pure before God? If it is not, ask God to wash you in His blood and renew your love for Him.

2. Does your "belief" in God seem weak or non-existent? Then take time today to talk to Him about how you desire to renew your spiritual walk with Him and be fully restored in your relationship with Him.

Journal: What Is God Saying to Me?- Date: _____

_____

_____

_____

_____

_____

_____

_____

_____

_____

_____

_____

_____

_____

Day 2: *True Confessions*

Scriptures:

"If we confess our sins, he is faithful and righteous to forgive us our sins, and to cleanse us from all unrighteousness." (1 John 1:9)

1. Open your heart to God today and spill your heart to Him confessing anything that brings conviction to your own heart knowing that these things displease the Lord's heart.

2. Be specific with your sins as much as you can. Sometimes it is a good idea to write down all the sins that the Holy Spirit recalls and then repent of each one of them as you write them.

Journal: What Is God Saying to Me? - Date: _____

_____

_____

_____

_____

_____

_____

_____

Day 3: *Walk in Forgiveness!*

Scriptures:

"**Repent therefore and be converted, that your sins may be blotted out, so that times of refreshing may come from the presence of the Lord...**" (Acts 3:19)

1. Ask yourself the following questions about forgiveness:
    a. Have I received forgiveness from God?
    b. Have I forgiven those who have offended me?
    c. Have I asked forgiveness from those who I have offended?

Journal: What Is God Saying to Me? - Date: _____

_____

_____

_____

_____

_____

_____

_____

_____

_____

_____

Day 4: *The Power of the Blood!*

Scriptures:

"In Him we have redemption through His blood, the forgiveness of sins, according to the riches of His grace..." (Ephesians 1:7)

1. After you repented and were washed in the blood of Jesus, do you still struggle with guilt, shame, or doubt about your new position in Christ?

2. Most of our experiences in the Lord and especially our confessions, are done by faith.

3. We must embrace what Jesus said - then we are to hold-on until the feelings and emotions come!

Journal: What Is God Saying to Me? - Date: _____

_____

_____

_____

_____

_____

_____

_____

Day 5: *An Attitude of the Kingdom!*

Scriptures:

"In the kingdom of God, eating and drinking are not important. The important things are living right with God, peace, and joy in the Holy Spirit." (Romans 14:17)

1. After you have confessed and know in your own heart that you have been forgiven, walk in that forgiveness! Let the joy of the Lord come forth and walk in thanksgiving, peace, and joy.

2. Always know that God is your Father, and He will always lead you in the right path.

Journal: What Is God Saying to Me? - Date:_____

_____
_____
_____
_____
_____
_____
_____
_____
_____

Day 6: *Have You Met the Accuser of the Bretheren?*

Scriptures:

"Then I heard a great voice in Heaven cry: "Now the salvation and the power and kingdom of our God, and the authority of his Christ have come! For the accuser of our brethren has been thrown down from this place, where he stood before our God accusing them day and night. Now they have conquered him through the blood of the Lamb, and through the Word to which they bore witness. They did not cherish life even in the face of death!" (Revelation 12:10 - Philips Translation)

1. The devil is known as the accuser of the Bretheren. His goal is to continually keep us under guilt and shame, boxed-in in failure!

2. When the accuser [the devil] comes to us, we must by faith, allow the Spirit of God to lift a standard against Him and re-enforce the power of the blood and how Christ has defeated him at the cross of Calvary.

3. Know that Christ also resurrected in bodily form after three days from the tomb. The devil

hates to hear this, so remind Him of this fact.

4. When the devil reminds you of your past – remind him of his future!

Journal: What Is God Saying to Me? - Date: _____

_____

_____

_____

_____

_____

_____

_____

_____

_____

_____

_____

Day 7: *If You Sin!*

Scriptures:

"My little children, these things I write to you, so that you may not sin. And if anyone sins, we have an Advocate with the Father, Jesus Christ the righteous. And He Himself is the propitiation for our sins, and not for ours only but also for the whole world." (1 John 2:1)

1. Just because you struggle with a certain sin, it doesn't mean that the game is over! The enemy is an expert at making you feel like a "loser!"

2. The enemy would love for you to quit on God at this very moment – but don't quit! Know that Jesus has forgiven you and you are on your way to victory!

3. Know that God has provided for you an Advocate to speak for you – His name is Jesus Christ. Talk to Him about your struggle, repent of any known sin, and enjoy His forgiveness.

4. He has promised to keep us to the very end!

Journal: What Is God Saying to Me? - Date: _____

_____

_____

_____

_____

_____

_____

_____

_____

_____

_____

_____

_____

A LIFE OF SURRENDER!

Day 8: *A Godly Desire!*

Scriptures:

"Then Jesus said to His disciples, "If anyone desires to come after Me, let him deny himself, and take up his cross, and follow Me." (Matthew 16:24)

1. Once a man or woman is born-again and washed in the precious blood of Jesus, they will enter God's kingdom. A life of surrender is then presented to that individual; to give their all for the sake of following Christ in the world he lives in.

2. The first part to Matthew 16:24, deals with the desire. Jesus said, "If anyone desires to come after Me...".

   A. The word desires in the Greek means, "to be inclined to; to consent to."
      [ ] Is there something inside of you that moves you deep within to follow Jesus?
      [ ] If you do - then follow your inclination!

Journal: What Is God Saying to Me? - Date: _____

_____

_____

_____

_____

_____

_____

_____

_____

_____

_____

_____

_____

Day 9: *Denying Self!*

Scriptures:

"Then Jesus said to His disciples, "If anyone desires to come after Me, let him deny himself, and take up his cross, and follow Me." (Matthew 16:24)

    1. Deny in Greek means, "to take something forcefully; to capture in war."

        A. To deny self means to take all our fleshly and selfish ideas and desires captive. as if in a war. Self must be taken by force. It will not leave any other way!

Journal: What Is God Saying to Me? - Date: _____

_____

_____

_____

_____

_____

_____

_____

_____

_____

Day 10: *Taking Up Your Cross!*

Scriptures:

"Then Jesus said to His disciples, "If anyone desires to come after Me, let him deny himself, and take up his cross, and follow Me." (Matthew 16:24)

1. "To take up or lift up a cross" in the Greek means, "obedience to the will of God declared by Jesus. It also signified readiness for self-denial and martyrdom in following Jesus."

   A. Is your heart to follow Jesus' even unto death? Evaluate your heart before God.

2. Always remember that a man who was carrying a cross outside the city gates was never coming back! You will never come back to your normal life after giving your heart to Jesus!

3. If you truly come to Jesus and give Him all your heart, know that you will be ruined for the ordinary!

Journal: What Is God Saying to Me? - Date: _____

_____

_____

_____

_____

_____

_____

_____

_____

_____

_____

_____

_____

Day 11: *An Exchanged Life!*

Scriptures:

"It is no longer I who live, but Christ (the Messiah) lives in me; and the life I now live in the body I live by faith in (by adherence to and reliance on and complete trust in) the Son of God..." (Galatians 2:20)

1. Do you understand Galatians 2:20? Have you surrendered your life to the point where you want what God wants?

2. Have you exchanged your life for His?

3. Have you surrendered your own plans and ambitions to God?

4. Have you embraced His will for your life?

Journal: What Is God Saying to Me? - Date:_____

_____

_____

_____

_____

_____

_____

_____

_____

_____

_____

_____

_____

_____

Day 12: *Not Living for Myself!*

Scriptures:

"...and He died for all, that those who live should live no longer for themselves, but for Him who died for them and rose again." (2 Corinthians 5:15)

1. The Christian life has to do with dying to self and embracing God's will.

2. Only as one surrenders their all to God, can they function as God's instruments in the world.

3. Are you allowing yourself to be God's instrument to touch the world?

Journal: What Is God Saying to Me? - Date: _____

_____

_____

_____

_____

_____

_____

_____

_____

_____

_____

_____

_____

_____

Day 13: *Have You Counted the Cost?*

Scriptures:

"For which of you, intending to build a tower, does not sit down first and count the cost, whether he has enough to finish it—lest, after he has laid the foundation, and is not able to finish, all who see it begin to mock him, saying, 'This man began to build and was not able to finish.'" (Luke 14:28)

1. Following Jesus is not cheap! Those who follow Him must first count the cost. It will cost you a lot – your very life!

2. Following Jesus is not on the FOR-SALE table!

3. Are you willing to pay whatever it takes to follow Him?

Journal: What Is God Saying to Me? Date: _____

_____

_____

_____

_____

_____

_____

_____

_____

_____

_____

_____

_____

_____

Day 14: *Freed to Follow!*

Scriptures:

"For he who has died has been freed from sin." (Romans 6:6)

1. Part of surrendering to Christ, is the fact of leaving the old self, the old nature behind. If one fails to understand that one must die to the flesh first, that individual will never think of surrendering wholly to Jesus!

2. Have you died to self?

3. Have you been freed from that sinful nature that once held you captive to its habits and ways?

Journal: What Is God Saying to Me? - Date: _____

_____

_____

_____

_____

_____

_____

_____

DEVELOPING AN EAR TO HEAR GOD!

Day 15: *Hearing God for Spiritual Repositioning!*

Scriptures:

"Now the LORD had said to Abram:
"Get out of your country,
From your family
And from your father's house,
To a land that I will show you.
I will make you a great nation;
I will bless you
And make your name great;
And you shall be a blessing.
I will bless those who bless you,
And I will curse him who curses you;
And in you all the families of the earth shall be blessed."
So, Abram departed as the LORD had spoken to him, and
Lot went with him." (Genesis 12:1-4)

1. We must learn to hear God and trust Him
   fully when the time comes to take steps into
   the future.

2. Moving with God into our future, sometimes

requires for us to let go of the things that tie us down to the present.

3. Always remember: You can't move forward if you are clinging to the present.

4. If God calls us to move, we move. If God tells us to stay, we stay!

Journal: What Is God Saying to Me? - Date: _____

_____

_____

_____

_____

_____

_____

_____

_____

_____

_____

_____

Day 16: *Hearing God for Developing Deeper Obedience!*

Scriptures:

"Now it came to pass after these things that God tested Abraham, and said to him, "Abraham!" And he said, "Here I am." Then He said, "Take now your son, your only son Isaac, whom you love, and go to the land of Moriah, and offer him there as a burnt offering on one of the mountains of which I shall tell you." So, Abraham rose early in the morning and saddled his donkey, and took two of his young men with him, and Isaac his son; and he split the wood for the burnt offering and arose and went to the place of which God had told him. Then on the third day Abraham lifted his eyes and saw the place afar off. And Abraham said to his young men, "Stay here with the donkey; the lad and I will go yonder and worship, and we will come back to you." So, Abraham took the wood of the burnt offering and laid it on Isaac his son; and he took the fire in his hand, and a knife, and the two of them went together. But Isaac spoke to Abraham his father and said, "My father!" And he said, "Here I am, my son." Then he said, "Look, the fire and the wood, but where is the lamb for a burnt offering?" And Abraham said, "My son, God will provide for Himself the lamb for a burnt offering." (Genesis 22:1-8)

1. There will be times when God will speak to us so that He may test our level of worship. Do we love Him more than anything else in our lives?

2. Are we willing to surrender all that is valuable to us, so that we may please Him? Evaluate this in your own walk with Him.

3. God desires that we be quick to hear Him and that we be quick to always obey Him. This is truly the call of those who want to follow Him closely.

4. Isaac symbolizes a possible idol in our own lives. Are we clinging to an idol or are we pledging our love to something or someone more than Jesus?

Journal: What Is God Saying to Me? - Date:_____

_____

_____

_____

_____

_____

_____

_____

_____

_____

_____

_____

_____

Day 17: *Learning to Hear God When Entering Holy Ground!*

Scriptures:

"Now Moses was tending the flock of Jethro his father-in-law, the priest of Midian. And he led the flock to the back of the desert, and came to Horeb, the mountain of God. And the Angel of the LORD appeared to him in a flame of fire from the midst of a bush. So, he looked, and behold, the bush was burning with fire, but the bush was not consumed. Then Moses said, "I will now turn aside and see this great sight, why the bush does not burn." So, when the LORD saw that he turned aside to look, God called to him from the midst of the bush and said, "Moses, Moses! And he said, "Here I am."
Then He said, "Do not draw near this place. Take your sandals off your feet, for the place where you stand is holy ground." (Exodus 3:1-5)

1. We never enter anything unless the Lord draws us or calls us there. Moses was called to see and experience God through the burning bush.

2. Are you listening to God's prompting and invitations to a deeper life in Him?

3. Taking off the sandals represented the yielding of one's personal rights. Have you surrendered your rights to Jesus?

4. Have you prayed: "God everything I have is yours," and truly meant it from the heart? Ponder this.

Journal: What Is God Saying to Me? - Date: _____

_____
_____
_____
_____
_____
_____
_____
_____
_____
_____
_____
_____
_____
_____

Day 18: *Hearing God When Feeling Unworthy!*

Scriptures:

"Now the Angel of the LORD came and sat under the terebinth tree, which was in Ophrah, which belonged to Joash the Abiezrite, while his son Gideon threshed wheat in the winepress, in order to hide it from the Midianites. And the Angel of the LORD appeared to him, and said to him, "The LORD is with you, you mighty man of valor!" Gideon said to Him, "O my lord, if the LORD is with us, why then has all this happened to us? And where are all His miracles which our fathers told us about, saying, 'Did not the LORD bring us up from Egypt?' But now the LORD has forsaken us and delivered us into the hands of the Midianites." Then the LORD turned to him and said, "Go in this might of yours, and you shall save Israel from the hand of the Midianites. Have I not sent you?" (Judges 6:1-6)

"But God has chosen the foolish things of the world to put to shame the wise, and God has chosen the weak things of the world to put to shame the things which are mighty..." (1 Corinthians 1:27)

1. When God called out Gideon, He didn't call

him because he was qualified, skillful, smart, or courageous. He called him because God needed a weak vessel that He could flow through. He needed a man that would yield to His voice and follow His commands. Gideon was that man!

2. Are you struggling with your own self-esteem?

3. Are you feeling unworthy to be used by God?

4. Do you feel disqualified? If you feel disqualified, then that qualifies you to be used by God. Don't let the devil tell you otherwise!

Journal: What Is God Saying to Me? - Date: _____

_____

_____

_____

_____

_____

_____

_____

_____

_____

_____

Day 19: *Hearing God When Entering Spiritual Battles!*

Scriptures:

"And David inquired of the LORD, saying, If I pursue after this troop, shall I overtake them? And he answered him, pursue for thou shalt surely overtake them, and shalt without fail recover all." (1 Samuel 30:8)

1. When in spiritual battles, it is wise for the servant of the Lord to turn to the Lord's voice for knowledge, wisdom, and strategy.

2. The servant of God must always be in touch with God and know what God's intentions are in any spiritual battle.

3. Too often God's servant will end-up committing spiritual shipwreck. What is the reason for this? The simple reason: he doesn't allow himself the time to listen to the voice of God during the battle. If you haven't figured it out yet, it is time: we are not that smart!

Journal: What Is God Saying to Me? - Date: _____

_____

Day 20: *Hearing God When in personal Economical Need!*

Scriptures:

"Then the word of the LORD came to him, saying, "Arise, go to Zarephath, which belongs to Sidon, and dwell there. See, I have commanded a widow there to provide for you." So he arose and went to Zarephath. And when he came to the gate of the city, indeed a widow was there gathering sticks. And he called to her and said, "Please bring me a little water in a cup, that I may drink." And as she was going to get it, he called to her and said, "Please bring me a morsel of bread in your hand." So, she said, "As the LORD your God lives, I do not have bread, only a handful of flour in a bin, and a little oil in a jar; and see, I am gathering a couple of sticks that I may go in and prepare it for myself and my son, that we may eat it, and die." And Elijah said to her, "Do not fear; go and do as you have said, but make me a small cake from it first, and bring it to me; and afterward make some for yourself and your son. For thus says the LORD God of Israel: 'The bin of flour shall not be used up, nor shall the jar of oil run dry, until the day the LORD sends rain on the earth.'" So, she went away and did according to the word of Elijah; and she and he and her household ate for many days. The bin of flour was not used up, nor did the jar of oil run dry, according to the word of the LORD which He spoke by Elijah." (1 Kings 17:8-16)

1. When in struggle with finances and daily provision:
   [ ] Give! Even if it's a small offering.
   [ ] Trust God with the little you have and watch it multiply.
   [ ] Don't hold back from blessing someone. (This is a trap to keep you in bondage and fear.)
   [ ] If you don't have a ministry or church you attend, then go and find a homeless man and buy him lunch and be a blessing in his life! This will set God's favor in motion on your behalf.

Journal: What Is God Saying to Me? - Date: _____

_____
_____
_____
_____
_____
_____
_____
_____
_____

Day 21: *Hearing God When He Is Inviting Us to Move with Him!*

Scriptures:

"On the same day, when evening had come, He said to them, "Let us cross over to the other side." Now when they had left the multitude, they took Him along in the boat as He was. And other little boats were also with Him. And a great windstorm arose, and the waves beat into the boat, so that it was already filling. But He was in the stern, asleep on a pillow. And they awoke Him and said to Him, "Teacher, do You not care that we are perishing?" Then He arose and rebuked the wind, and said to the sea, "Peace, be still!" And the wind ceased and there was a great calm. But He said to them, "Why are you so fearful? How is it that you have no faith?" And they feared exceedingly, and said to one another, "Who can this be, that even the wind and the sea obey Him!" (Mark 4:35-41)

1. God knows our spiritual strength and level of faith.

2. Any time He invites us to take a walk with Him, it is an invitation to grow in Him!

3. Following Jesus produces opportunities for spiritual growth and maturity.

4. Following Christ is not a popular thing to do in our day and age. So those who follow Him, they truly do it because they love Him and want to know Him deeper.

Journal: What Is God Saying to Me? Date: _____

_____
_____
_____
_____
_____
_____
_____
_____
_____
_____
_____
_____
_____

WALKING IN REAL FAITH!

Day 22: *What Is Faith?*

Scriptures:

"NOW FAITH is the assurance (the confirmation, the title deed) **of the things** [we] **hope for, being the proof of things** [we] **do not see and the conviction of their reality** [faith perceiving as real fact what is not revealed to the senses]**."** (Hebrews 11:1 - Amplified Version)

1. Faith is not wishful thinking! Faith may be blind to our flesh, but not to our spirit!

2. Too many people think that faith is something you find within your own self and declare it to be God.

3. Faith has two sides to it: metaphysical and spiritual. Too many believers are walking in the flesh moving in metaphysical faith. This is a faith that is carnal birthed out of our own intellect.

4. Real faith, mountain-moving faith, that heavenly f

faith Jesus spoke of when He said we needed a little of, the mustard-seed faith – can only be deposited by God into our inner man. You are not born with this faith; the Lord Himself gives it as He sees fit.

5. Make sure that when you make decrees, declarations, or pray back a prophetic promise, word, or dream; make sure it was deposited into your spirit by God! Be aware and make sure you are not moving in fleshly wishful thinking!

6. The Scripture above also says to us that **"now faith is!"**

7. This means that faith is now. In other words, when God tells you something or makes a promise to you, faith has been activated in heaven! All we must to do is believe what God told us and walk it out as someone who has just received a "title deed" to that promise. It is as good as done!

8. One thing is to force ourselves to believe something God never spoke into our spiritual

being; but it is totally another thing when God deposits faith into us and we believe.

9. As you move with God through this fast, ask yourself, "Am I following Christ by faith?" "Am I by faith, trusting Him with my finances, my family, my ministry, my business?" Has He given me a "title deed" regarding my family, my business, my ministry, etc.?

Journal: What Is God Saying to Me?-Date: _____

_____

_____

_____

_____

_____

_____

_____

_____

_____

_____

_____

Day 23: *Without Faith It is Impossible!*

Scriptures:

"But without faith it is impossible to please Him, for he who comes to God must believe that He is, and that He is a rewarder of those who diligently seek Him." (Hebrews 11:6)

1. The Scripture is very clear about a matter here: It reads, "Without faith, it is impossible to please Him..."

2. What does this verse say to you? (Please share your thoughts below.)

Journal: What Is God Saying to Me? - Date: _____

_____

_____

_____

_____

_____

_____

_____

_____

_____

_____

_____

Day 24: *Real Faith IS God's Economy!*

Scriptures:

"But without faith it is impossible to please Him, for he who comes to God must believe that He is, and that He is a rewarder of those who diligently seek Him." (Hebrews 11:6)

1. Faith is the currency of the kingdom of God.

2. God will always reward those who diligently seek Him or trust Him.

3. How much of this real faith do you presently possess?

4. You see, without faith we can't . . .
   a. See God moving.
   b. Feel God moving.
   c. Hear God leading.
   d. Taste God's goodness.
   e. Experience His beauty.
   f. Simply put, we can't even please Him!

Journal: What Is God Saying to Me? - Date: _____

_____

_____

_____

_____

_____

_____

_____

_____

_____

_____

_____

_____

_____

Day 25: *The Faith OF God VS. Faith IN God.*

Scriptures:

"Now in the morning, as they passed by, they saw the fig tree dried up from the roots. And Peter, remembering, said to Him, "Rabbi, look! The fig tree which You cursed has withered away." So, Jesus answered and said to them, "Have faith in God. For assuredly, I say to you, whoever says to this mountain, 'Be removed and be cast into the sea,' and does not doubt in his heart, but believes that those things he says will be done, he will have whatever he says. Therefore, I say to you, whatever things you ask when you pray, believe that you receive them, and you will have them." (Mark 11:20-24)

1. In this specific verse, Jesus tells the disciples after seeing the withered fig tree: "Have faith in God." The correct interpretation in the original language has it, "Have faith OF God," not IN God.

2. My friends, the faith OF God is what we need within us. We get this type of faith downloaded in us by asking God for it.

3. Having faith IN God, is not the same as having the faith OF God.

    a. Having faith IN God simply means that we acknowledge His existence and involvement in our lives.

    b. Having faith OF God means that we become carriers of the same heavenly substance that God has, and this faith moves Him to act on our behalf here on earth.

Journal: What Is God Saying to Me? - Date: _____

_____

_____

_____

_____

_____

_____

_____

_____

_____

_____

_____

_____

Day 26: *Having the Faith of God When Nothing Is
Happening!*

Scriptures:

"Then He got into one of the boats, which was Simon's,
and asked him to put out a little from the land. And He
sat down and taught the multitudes from the boat. When
He had stopped speaking, He said to Simon, "Launch out
into the deep and let down your nets for a catch." But Simon answered and said to Him, "Master, we have toiled
all night and caught nothing; nevertheless, at Your word
I will let down the net." And when they had done this,
they caught a great number of fish, and their net was
breaking." (Mark 5:3-6)

1. Trying to make things happen in our own
   strength will only end in unproductivity and
   disappointment.

2. Sometimes we try to fix a situation in a
   particular area in our lives to no avail. Though
   we try and try, our good efforts as good as they
   may be, won't get it done. Why not?

3. I believe that some things are reserved for the

COME AWAY MY BELOVED!

revelation of God. The Lord desires to teach us His strategy, His perfect ways, etc.

4. Let us lend ourselves to the Lord's voice – He will instruct us accordingly.

Journal: What Is God Saying to Me? - Date: _____

_____

_____

_____

_____

_____

_____

_____

_____

_____

_____

_____

_____

Day 27: *Pressing Into What You Know Is Yours!*

Scriptures:

"And suddenly, a woman who had a flow of blood for twelve years came from behind and touched the hem of His garment. For she said to herself, "If only I may touch His garment, I shall be made well." But Jesus turned around, and when He saw her, He said, "Be of good cheer, daughter; your faith has made you well." And the woman was made well from that hour." (Matthew 9:20-22)

1. Sometimes the faith of God is deposited in our hearts, and we know that we know, God has done something deep within.

2. Though externally we may not see the results yet, we know in our hearts that it is coming and coming soon. This is the faith of God at work.

3. I believe that this woman with the issue of blood knew in her heart that her healing was about to come, and when Jesus showed up, she jumped to the opportunity not caring what anyone thought of her.

4. This is the attitude we should walk in for the rest of our days!

Journal: What Is God Saying to Me? - Date: _____

_____

_____

_____

_____

_____

_____

_____

_____

_____

_____

_____

_____

Day 28: *Unbelief Must Be Put Off and Out!*

Scriptures:

"When Jesus came into the ruler's house and saw the flute players and the noisy crowd wailing, He said to them, "Make room, for the girl is not dead, but sleeping." And they ridiculed Him. But when the crowd was put outside, He went in and took her by the hand, and the girl arose. And the report of this went out into all that land." (Matthew 9:3-6)

1. Real Faith has an enemy! It's a very powerful enemy. It is called unbelief!

2. Unbelief is so powerful that those who are possessed by it, will not see God at work. So, guess what? Unbelief must be put off and out of our sphere.

3. How do we do this? We must put out of our lives: television programs, magazines, books, YouTube videos, and social media that goes against the faith of God. Also, there are people that surround us daily who are not people of faith – they must go!

4. Real Faith can be generated as we yield ourselves to the Holy Spirit's leadership. Prayer, fasting, and the Reading of God's Word, will get us ablaze in God!

Journal: What Is God Saying to Me? - Date: _____

_____

_____

_____

_____

_____

_____

_____

_____

_____

_____

_____

_____

WALKING IN THE SPIRIT!

Day 29: *Cultivating the Fruit of the Spirit* - Love & Joy.

Scriptures:

"But the fruit of the Spirit is love, joy, peace, longsuffering, kindness, goodness, faithfulness, gentleness, self-control." (Galatians 5:22, 23)

1. Always keep in mind that the fruit of the Spirit is imparted into our hearts by God's Spirit - but must be developed daily.

2. Every experience that you and I face, will be an opportunity to develop the fruit of the Spirit in our lives.

3. Unlike the gifts of the Spirit, the fruit of the Spirit is something that must be intentionally cultivated and developed.

4. There is no easy way to learn on how to walk in the fruit of the Spirit; one must make the choice as he or she is daily challenged.

The first fruit of the Spirit that is on Paul's list is LOVE. What is LOVE? Love here is a strong positive emotion of regard and emotion. We must get to the place where we are moving in love daily. We must learn to apply this love in all areas of our life. We must learn to see love from God's perspective and not from a human-led and conditional type of love. His love was unconditional, and we must make it our aim to have the same kind of love.

[ ] Has your love developed in the sense that it has become unconditional just like Jesus' love?

[ ] Do you find it a struggle to love the "unlovable?"

[ ] If you don't love yourself, you won't love anyone else! Dwell on this and bring it before God.

The second fruit we see on Paul's list is the cultivation of JOY. What is JOY? The New Testament says that joy is the emotion of great happiness and pleasure. Now the Old Testament (Hebrew) brings to light the word joy as the reward for faithfulness to the Law in Is. 65:13 f.; Prv. 10:28. In other words, when we are walking in and under God's divine order, joy will flood our hearts. In Galatians 5, Paul is telling us to walk in divine order, so that joy can flood our hearts daily.

1. Are you walking in the joy of the Lord? The joy of the Lord has nothing to do with silly smiles and outrageous laughter; it has to do with our

alignment with God's heart and will. If we are walking in God's will, we will have joy!

Journal: What Is God Saying to Me? - Date: _____

_____

_____

_____

_____

_____

_____

_____

_____

_____

_____

_____

_____

Day 30: *Cultivating the Fruit of the Spirit* - Peace &
Longsuffering.

Scriptures:

**"But the fruit of the Spirit is love, joy, peace, longsuf-
fering, kindness, goodness, faithfulness, gentleness,
self-control."** (Galatians 5:22, 23)

Here's a couple more of the fruits of the Spirit as listed by the
Apostle Paul. Let us begin where we left off with the fruit
of PEACE. What is PEACE? Peace is not just two people
getting along, it is deeper than that; peace is a state of being at peace. Knowing that you are not at war or in conflict
with someone, brings about peace. Paul says that to have this
state of peace is a fruit that can be developed. To have a state
of peace upon you is truly remarkable and will be emulated
by others as they see the tranquility that surrounds you.

1. Are you at peace with God?

2. Are you at peace with yourself?

3. Are you at peace with others?

Another fruit listed is LONGSUFFERING. What is LONG-

SUFFERING? Longsuffering is patient endurance of pain or unhappiness. In the original idea of longsuffering, the Apostle Paul is depicting a picture of this word. What the Apostle Paul has in mind is that longsuffering is the the steadfastness of the general or soldier in putting up with hardships, i.e., "endurance" until a goal is reached. Or as a verb found in the same sense when those engaged in the battle of life are compared to swimmers in the sea who seek safety on the shore.

1. Do you easily give up when going "uphill" in life?

2. Do you quickly change your course simple because things get hard on you; or for not getting what you want or desire?

3. Longsuffering is such a needed fruit for any person who believes in His future!

Journal: What Is God Saying to Me? - Date: _____

_____

_____

_____

_____

_____

_____

_____

Day 31: *Cultivating the Fruit of the Spirit -* **Kindness.**

Scriptures:

"But the fruit of the Spirit is love, joy, peace, longsuf-fering, kindness, goodness, faithfulness, gentleness, self-control." (Galatians 5:22, 23)

Let us look at the fruit of KINDNESS. What did the Apostle Paul mean when he listed KINDNESS as a fruit. What is KINDNESS? Kindness is the quality of being warmhearted, considerate, humane, gentle, and sympathetic. There is a warmheartedness that comes inside of us when the Holy Spirit takes over our lives. This is definitely fruit we must recognize and cultivate within our hearts.

1. Have you found this fruit operating in your own life?
2. Sometimes God allows challenges to come our way where we must put to practice this type of kindness. Learn to recognize the Lord at work and making the opportunity available so that we may cultivate this godly kindness.

Journal: What Is God Saying to Me? - Date: _____

_____

Day 32: *Cultivating the Fruit of the Spirit -* **Goodness.**

Scriptures:

"But the fruit of the Spirit is love, joy, peace, longsuffering, kindness, goodness, faithfulness, gentleness, self-control." (Galatians 5:22, 23)

GOODNESS. From Paul's perspective, he also listed GOODNESS as a fruit of the Spirit. What does GOODNESS mean in its original context. The word GOODNESS means the quality of moral excellence, especially as a quality that is not stagnant, but actively working itself out. The opposite of this would be a person who is full of himself or someone with a big ego.

People who walk in the Spirit, are people who continually work at becoming more and more like Jesus. They are not content with what they have attained thus far; they are also people who don't sit back due to failure(s). They rise from the ashes and pursue the heart of God no matter what. Goodness is their goal!

1. Are you a person who has stopped growing because of failure?

2. Are you an individual who is too proud to see anything wrong in yourself?

Journal: What Is God Saying to Me? - Date: _____

_____

_____

_____

_____

_____

_____

_____

_____

_____

_____

_____

_____

_____

Day 33: *Cultivating the Fruit of the Spirit* - **Faithfulness.**

Scriptures:

"But the fruit of the Spirit is love, joy, peace, longsuffering, kindness, goodness, faithfulness, gentleness, self-control." (Galatians 5:22, 23)

Let us dip into the fruit of FAITHFULNESS. Faithfulness in this text means the quality of being faithful. It goes deeper still – it also bears out the qualities of a faithful individual such as confidence, trust. Also, a person who is trustworthy or reliable. Finally, someone who brings assurance.

This fruit is so important to cultivate and develop if God is ever going to use us in some way in His kingdom. You see, one must be full of faithfulness before He can be entrusted with keys of authority.

1. As a servant of God, do people have confidence in you? Do they trust you?

2. Have you proven yourself to be trustworthy or reliable in the small things?

3. Do you bring assurance to another individual,

to your family, to your company, your job or ministry?

Journal: What Is God Saying to Me? - Date: _____

_____

_____

_____

_____

_____

_____

_____

_____

_____

_____

_____

Day 34: *Cultivating the Fruit of the Spirit -* **Gentleness.**

Scriptures:

"But the fruit of the Spirit is love, joy, peace, longsuffering, kindness, goodness, faithfulness, gentleness, self-control." (Galatians 5:22, 23)

We have covered quite a bit in the fruit of the Spirit and there is a reason for me sharing these thoughts with you. If we can't get a hold of what the Spirit is doing WITHIN us, we might as well forget what He wants to do THROUGH us!

Let us study now the fruit of GENTLENESS. This word means to act in a manner that is gentle, mild, and even-tempered.

A person who has allowed God to deal with them, especially in character, will quickly develop this type of godly gentleness. To do the opposite of what the fruit of the Spirit is, would be an individual who is typically easily irritated and immediately loses control of their emotions. Meekness; gentleness; and mild-mannered individuals tend to be walking in the fruit and spirit of gentleness.

   1. When was the last time that you lost your

control, and your emotions got the best of you and left you repenting of it or asking for forgiveness from someone?

2. Gentleness is truly a characteristic of a mature individual.

Journal: What Is God Saying to Me? - Date:_____

_____

_____

_____

_____

_____

_____

_____

_____

_____

_____

_____

Day **35**: *Cultivating the Fruit of the Spirit* – Self-Control.

Scriptures:

"But the fruit of the Spirit is love, joy, peace, longsuffering, kindness, goodness, faithfulness, gentleness, self-control." (Galatians 5:22, 23)

Finally, as we come to the last of the fruits of the Spirit listed here in Galatians, let us look at SELF-CONTROL. What is SELF-CONTROL? Self-control denotes power or lordship, and expresses the power or lordship which one has either over oneself or over something. Did you get this?

This word has to do with having the power or the lordship ability to say NO to self! When in temptation, in testing, in a crisis, in difficulty, in decision-making mode – will you stay in Christ and do what Jesus would do OR will you do what your flesh desires to do?

1. Self-control is needed to be able to pursue God's will. God's will is definitely not man's will.

2. Are you strong enough to choose God and not your fleshly desires?

Journal: What Is God Saying to Me? - Date: _____

_____

_____

_____

_____

_____

_____

_____

_____

_____

_____

_____

_____

IN THE VISIONS OF GOD!

Day 36: *Make Sure Your Vision Was Initiated by God!*

Scriptures:

"Now the LORD had said to Abram:
"Get out of your country,
From your family
And from your father's house,
To a land that I will show you.
I will make you a great nation;
I will bless you
And make your name great;
And you shall be a blessing.
I will bless those who bless you,
And I will curse him who curses you;
And in you all the families of the earth shall be blessed."
So, Abram departed as the LORD had spoken to him..."
(Genesis 12:1-4)

1. The Lord is the giver of vision. All vision starts in His heart and shares it with ours.

2. If God gives us vision, we can be sure that He will show us how to walk it out.

3. Never make big consequential moves that God didn't initiate and then expect Him to bless it!

4. Abraham was led by God to move to a land that He would later show him. It was God who imparted this into His spirit-man.

5. Our lives are all about the Lord and His wishes, not ours!

Journal: What Is God Saying to Me? - Date: _____

_____

_____

_____

_____

_____

_____

_____

_____

_____

_____

_____

Day 37: *God Will Sustain His Vision!*

Scriptures:

"After these things the word of the LORD came to Abram in a vision, saying, "Do not be afraid, Abram. I am your shield, your exceedingly great reward." But Abram said, "Lord GOD, what will You give me, seeing I go childless, and the heir of my house is Eliezer of Damascus?" Then Abram said, "Look, You have given me no offspring; indeed one born in my house is my heir!" And behold, the word of the LORD came to him, saying, "This one shall not be your heir, but one who will come from your own body shall be your heir." Then He brought him outside and said, "Look now toward heaven, and count the stars if you are able to number them." And He said to him, "So shall your descendants be." (Genesis 15:1-5)

1. After God gives us vision, He alone is the one who sustains that vision.

2. Sometimes, we feel that He has given us a vision and then abandons us to deal with it all by ourselves. This is not the case.

3. Though sometimes, we feel like nothing is

happening, He will appear again and re-ignite that vision in our hearts!

4. If God called you to do something, He will bring it to pass.

Journal: What Is God Saying to Me? - Date: _____

_____
_____
_____
_____
_____
_____
_____
_____
_____
_____
_____
_____

Day 38: *God Open My Eyes to See!*

Scriptures:

"And when the servant of the man of God arose early and went out, there was an army, surrounding the city with horses and chariots. And his servant said to him, "Alas, my master! What shall we do?" So, he answered, "Do not fear, for those who are with us are more than those who are with them." And Elisha prayed, and said, "LORD, I pray, open his eyes that he may see." Then the LORD opened the eyes of the young man, and he saw. And behold, the mountain was full of horses and chariots of fire all around Elisha." (2 Kings 6:15-17)

1. Seeing the invisible realm, is one of the greatest benefits for any spirit-filled believer.

2. If you feel that your life is stagnant, ask God to show you. If you feel that your life is out of place – ask God to show you.

3. If you feel that God has something in store for you or your future, ask God to show you.

4. I believe the Lord wants us to see His blueprint

for our lives just as He designed it.

5. When in spiritual battle; when fear comes; when you feel trapped and overwhelmed; ask God to open your eyes! He will.

Journal: What Is God Saying to Me? - Date: _____

_____

_____

_____

_____

_____

_____

_____

_____

_____

_____

_____

_____

Day 39: *Living the Ascended Life!*

Scriptures:

"But God, who is rich in mercy, because of His great love with which He loved us, even when we were dead in trespasses, made us alive together with Christ (by grace you have been saved), and raised us up together, and made us sit together in the heavenly places in Christ Jesus..." (Ephesians 2:4-6)

1. Being in Jesus is having a mindset of victory; a mindset that teaches us that we are now seated with Him in heavenly places!

2. When the devil comes in like a roaring lion seeking to devour us (1 Peter 5:8), he can't find us. Why not? Because we are not in his realm (fleshly realm) – we are in God's realm (in the spirit, seated in heavenly places.).

3. When Christ made us alive in Him, He raised us up together and made us sit together in the heavenly places in Christ Jesus! This is a fact!

4. We rule over our thoughts from God's perspective,

and it doesn't matter what the devil wants to do!

5. We don't look up at a situation; we look down at it.

6. We must learn to live and move and have our being in this fundamental truth: We live in the heavenly places in Christ Jesus!

Journal: What Is God Saying to Me? - Date: _____

_____

_____

_____

_____

_____

_____

_____

_____

_____

_____

_____

_____

Day 40: *Jesus Commands Us to Go!*

Scriptures:

"And Jesus came and spoke to them, saying, "All authority has been given to Me in heaven and on earth. Go therefore and make disciples of all the nations, baptizing them in the name of the Father and of the Son and of the Holy Spirit, teaching them to observe all things that I have commanded you; and lo, I am with you always, even to the end of the age." Amen. (Matthew 28:18-20)

1. We must be quick to hear and quick to obey Him!

2. Jesus said "Go!" This was the Great Commission NOT the Great Suggestion!

3. We must develop an outreach-oriented mindset of Christianity.

4. Let your outreach be both LOCAL and GLOBAL. People need Jesus across the street from where we live as well as across the ocean in foreign lands.

5. God has equipped with us with the ability and talent to have an impact with our lives. Simply

by obeying His Word, we will be held accountable by what He told us to do before He left.

Journal: What Is God Saying to Me? - Date: _____

_____

_____

_____

_____

_____

_____

_____

_____

_____

_____

_____

_____

Ministry Information & Resources

For the purchase of more books from David Mayorga, feel free to visit our online store at:
www.shabarpublications.com
www.amazon.com

For more ministry information or ministry training through conferences or seminars; or for speaking engagements, please feel free to email David Mayorga at
mayorga1126@gmail.com.

Donations can be made to:
www.masterbuildertx.com/donate

All donations made to Masterbuilder Ministries
are *tax exempt.*

Thank You!

www.ingramcontent.com/pod-product-compliance
Lightning Source LLC
Chambersburg PA
CBHW071359120626
46546CB00002B/749